Inspirational Coloring Books For Girls

THIS BOOK

BELONGS TO

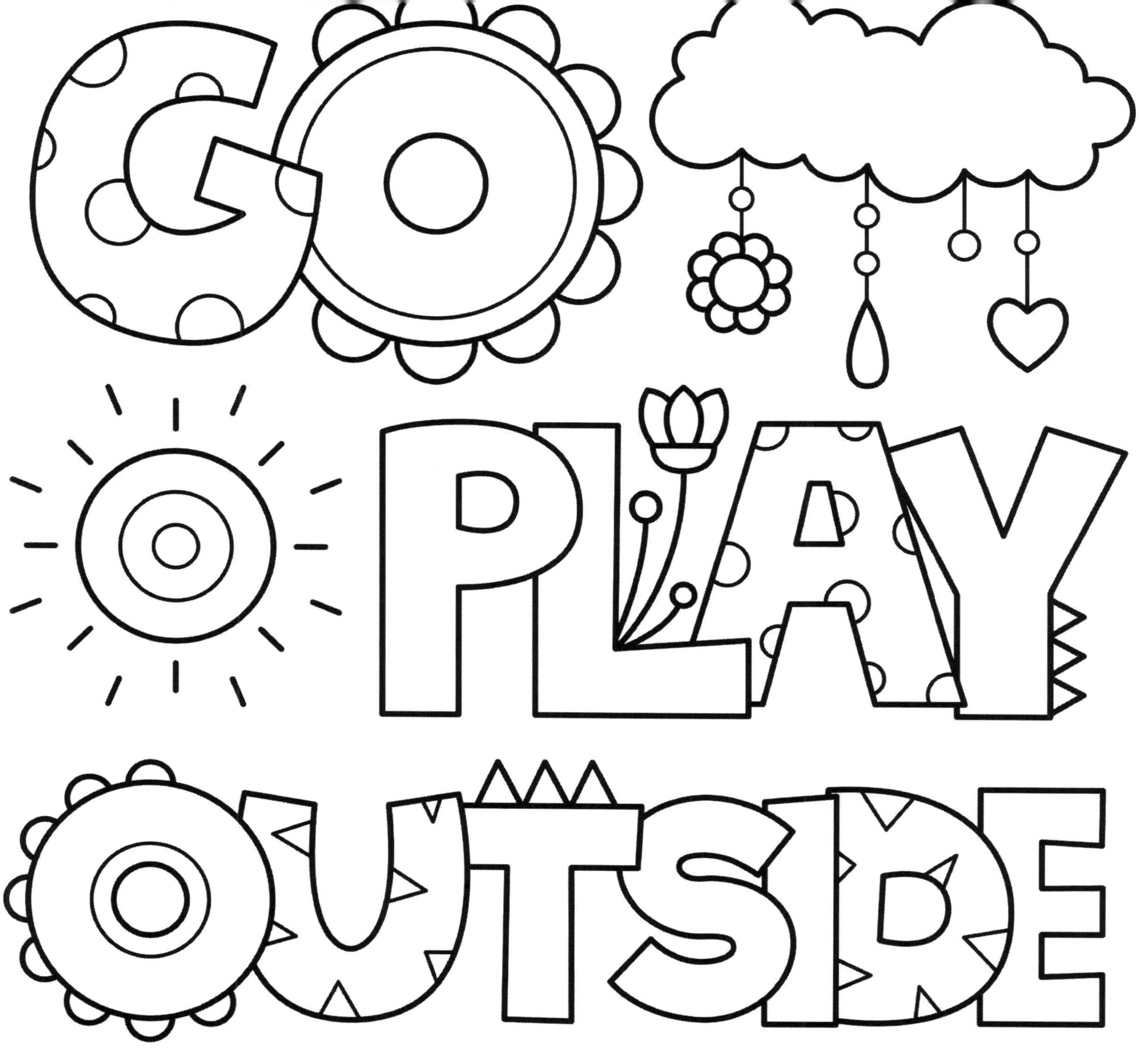
GO
PLAY
OUTSIDE

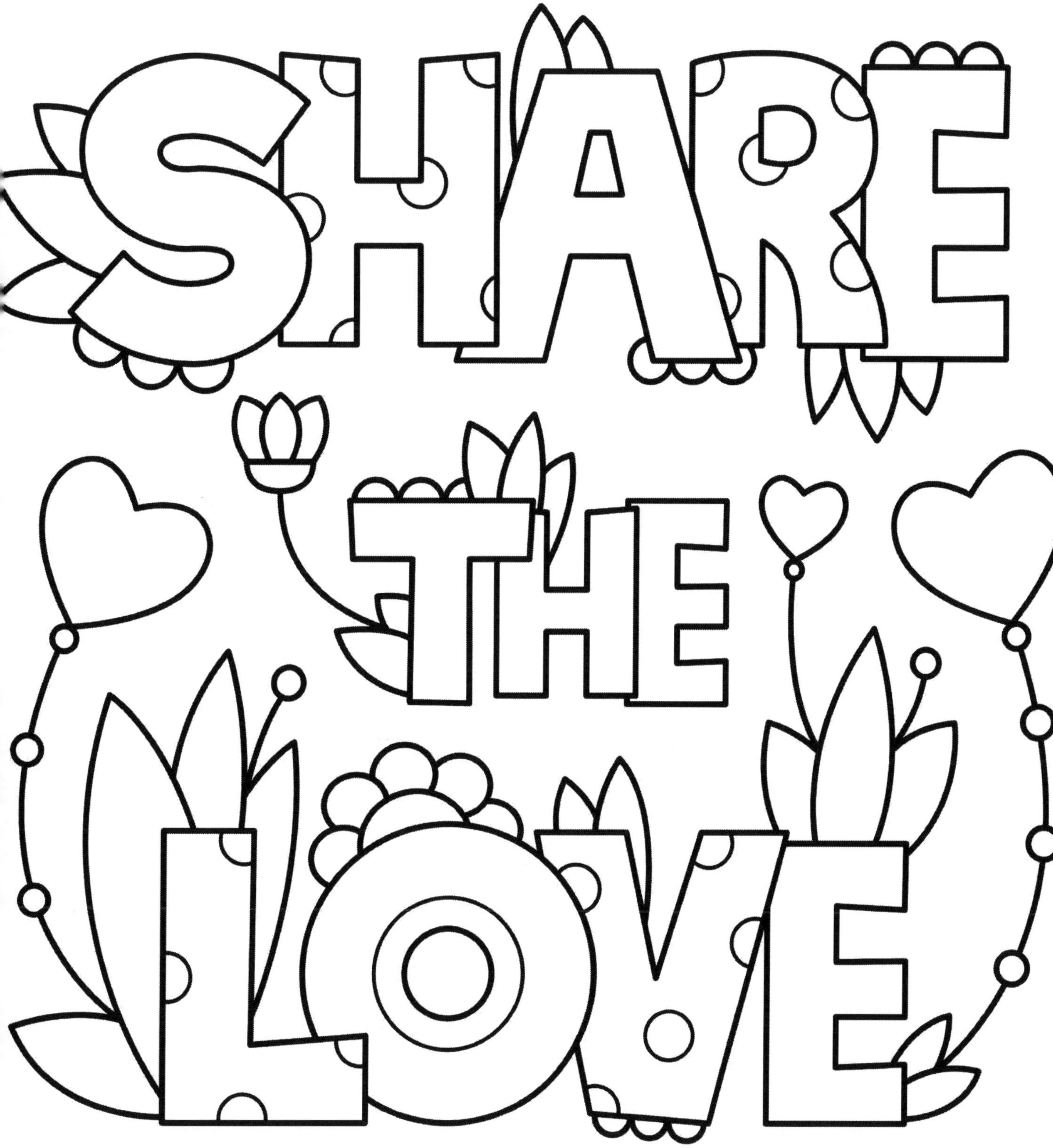
SHARE
THE
LOVE

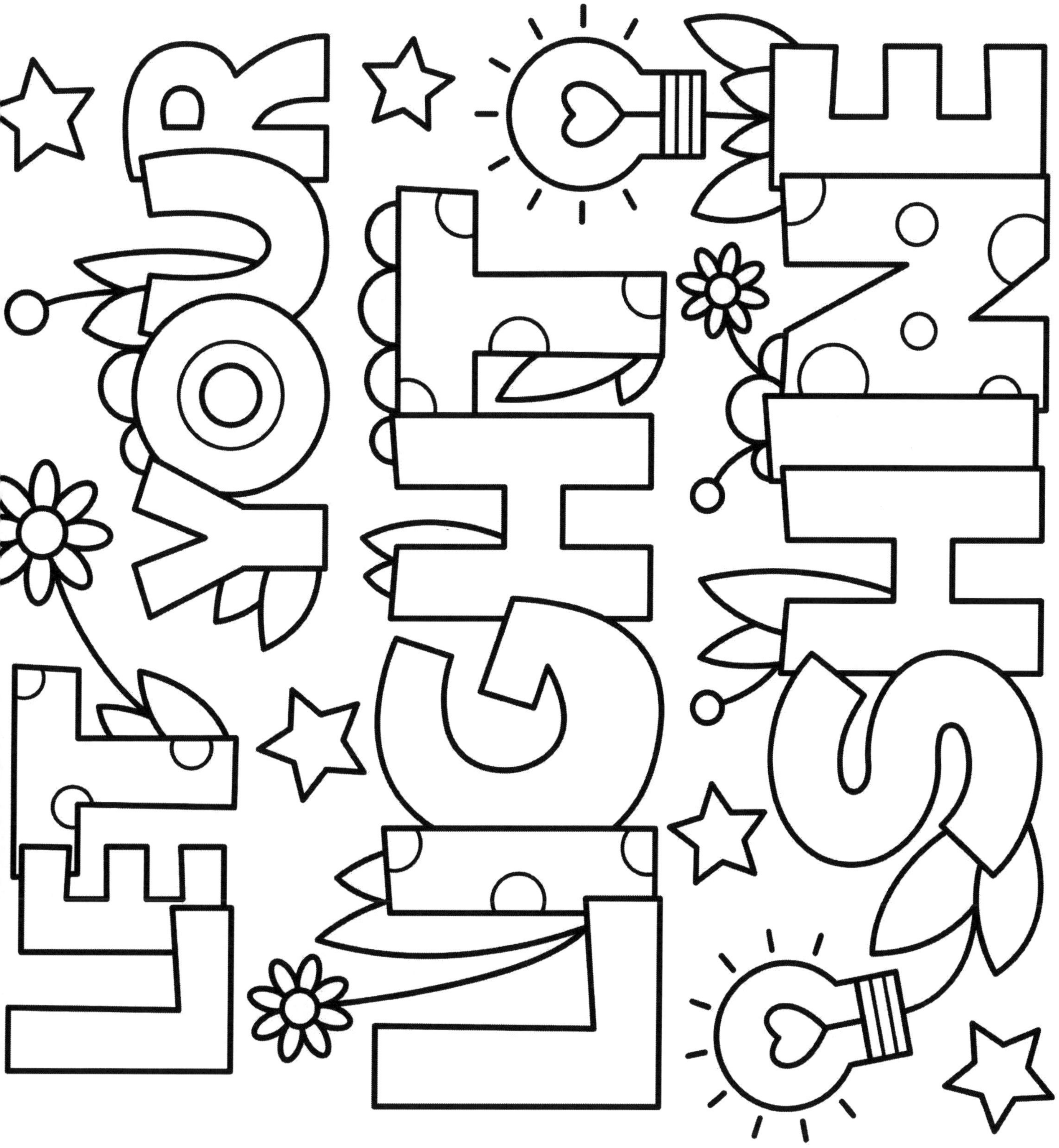
LET YOUR LIGHT SHINE

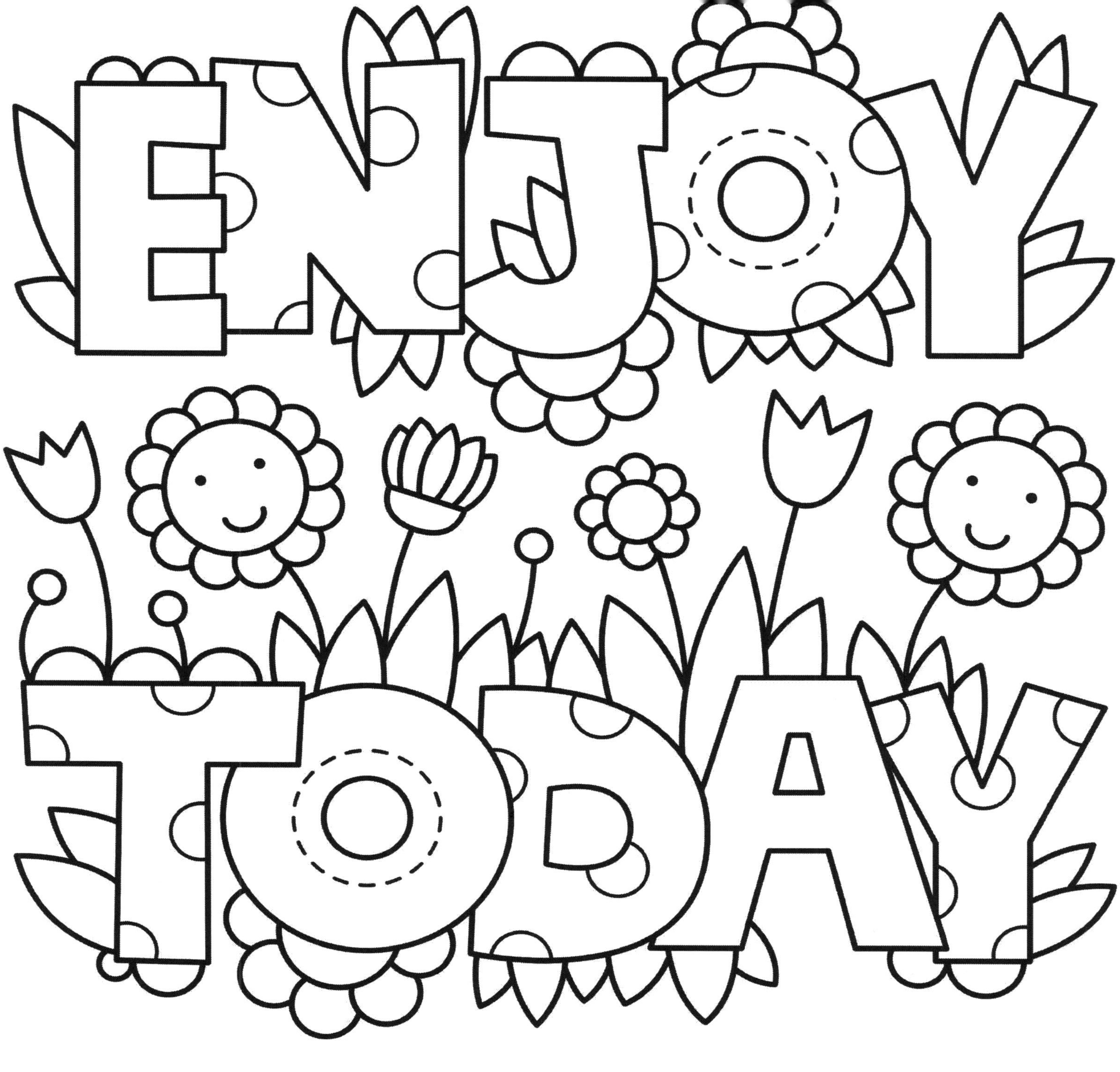
ENJOY
TODAY

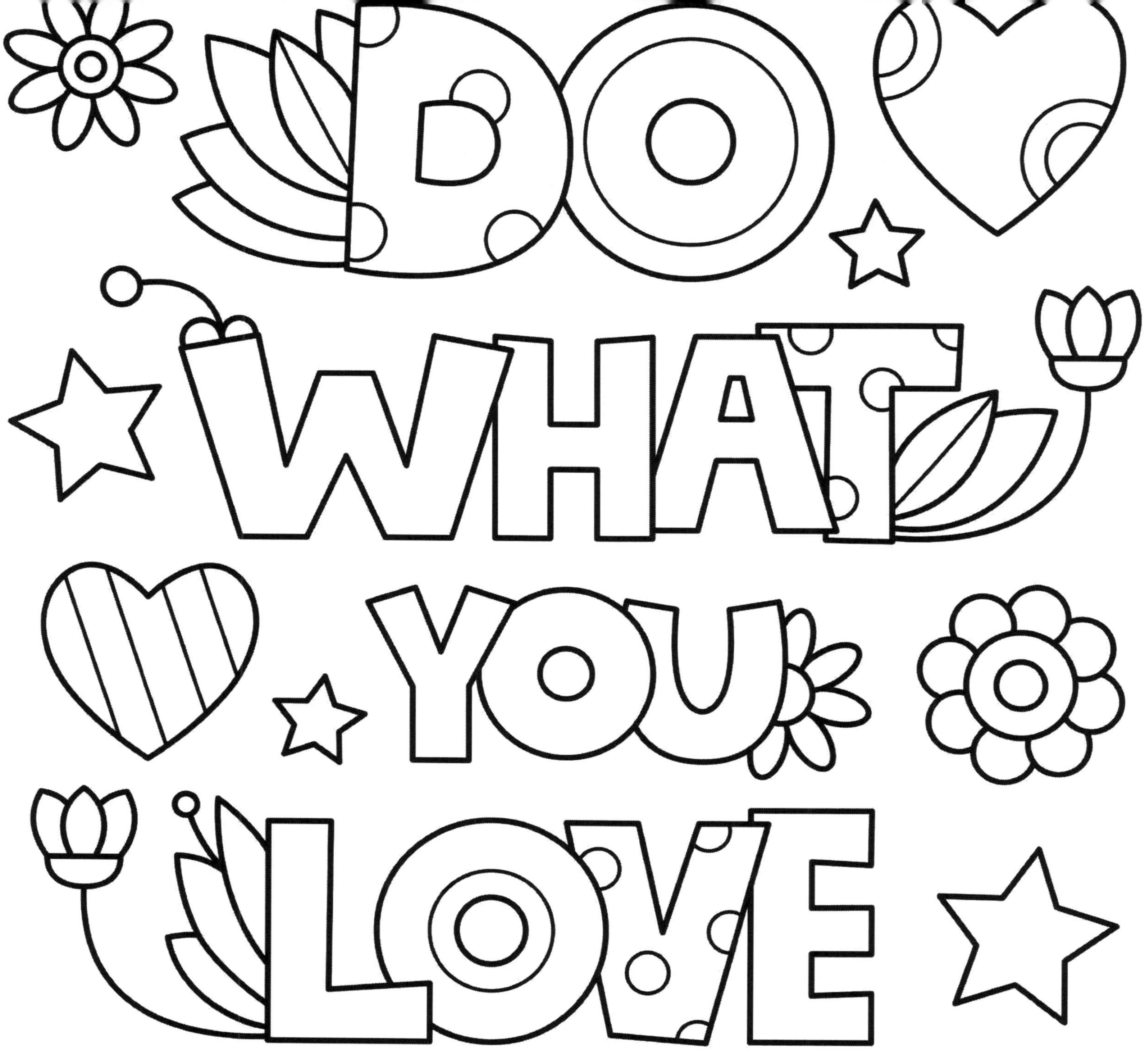
DO
WHAT
YOU
LOVE

LET YOUR LIGHT SHINE

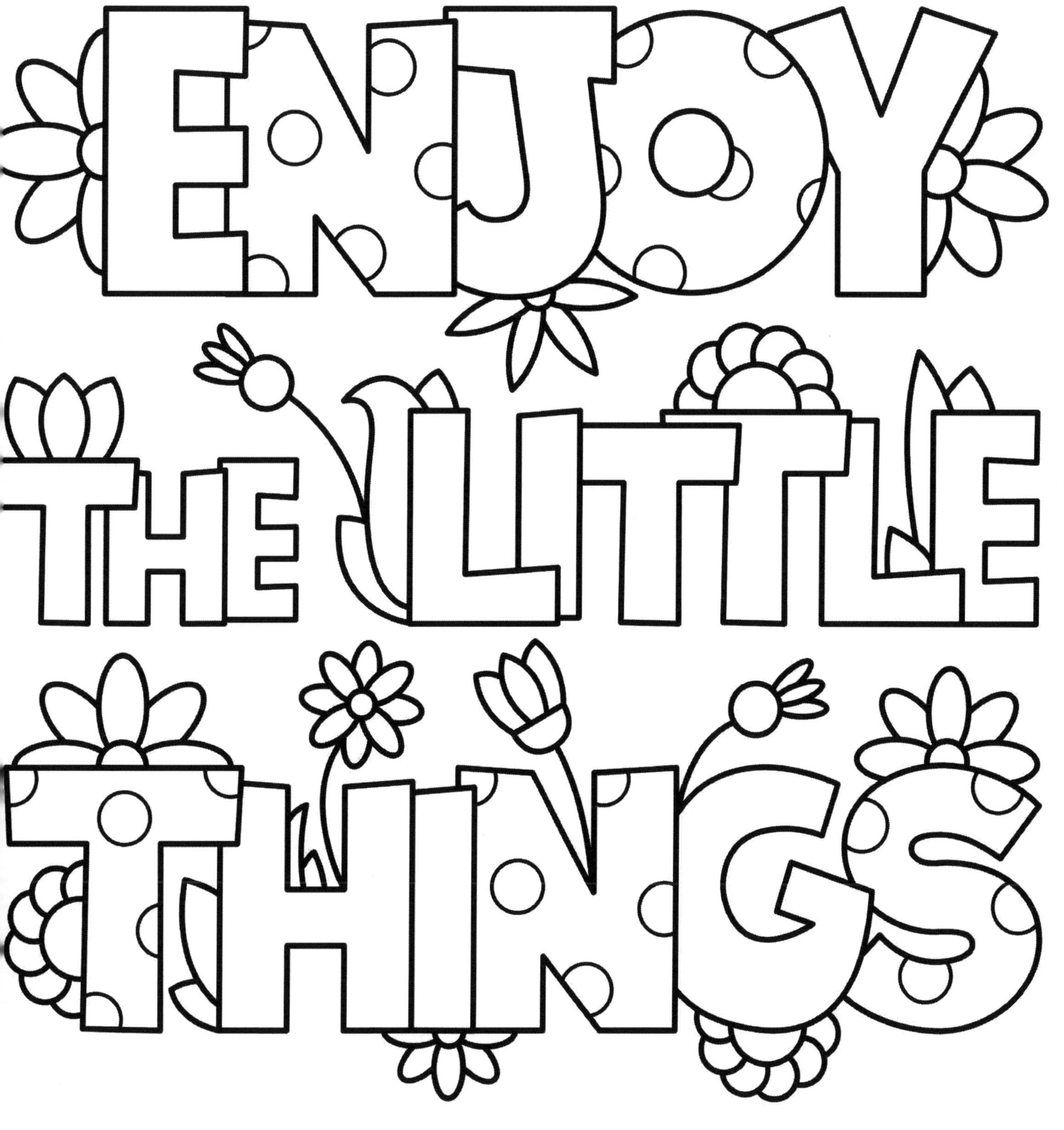
ENJOY
THE LITTLE
THINGS

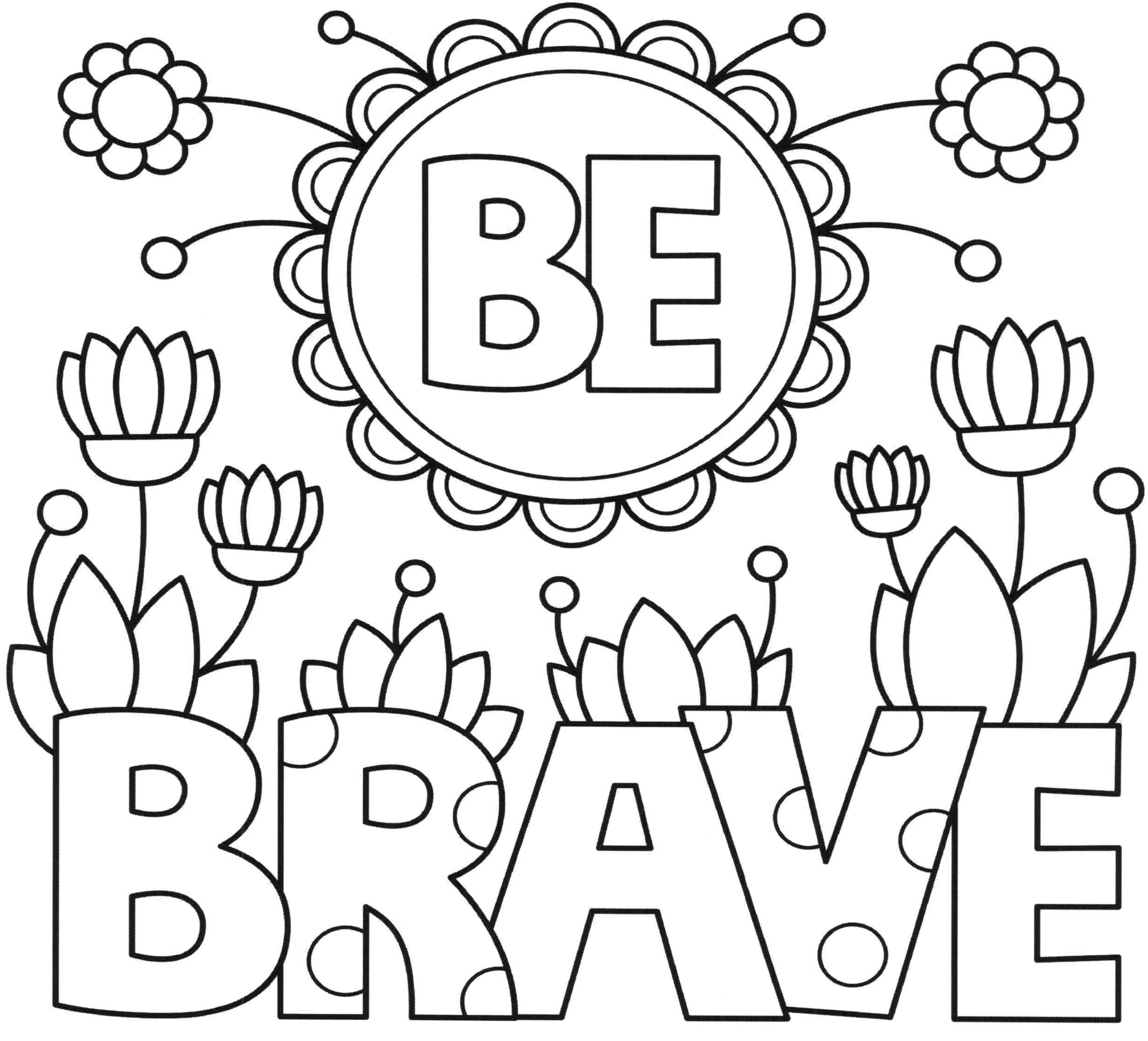
BE
BRAVE

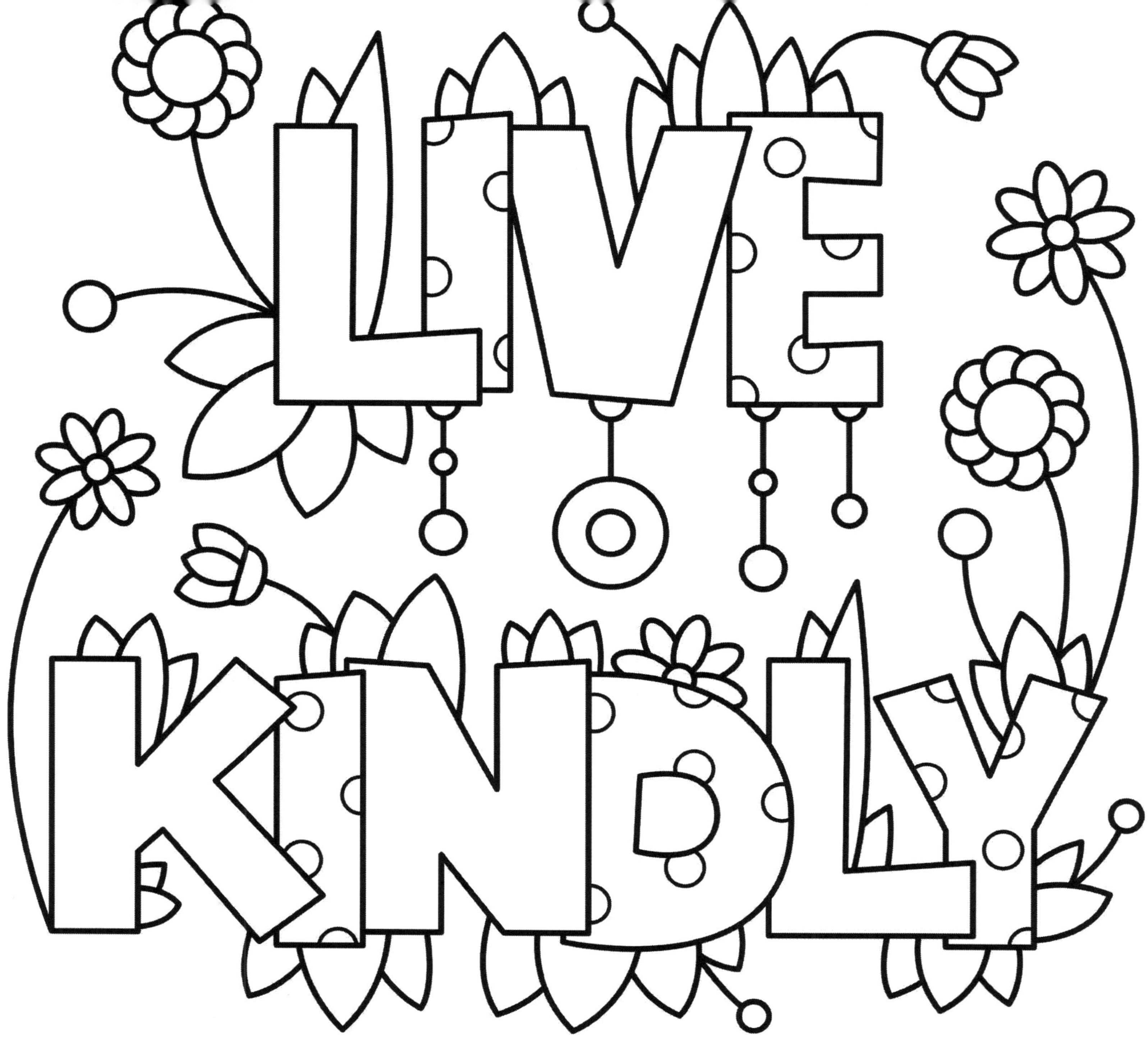
LIVE
KINDLY

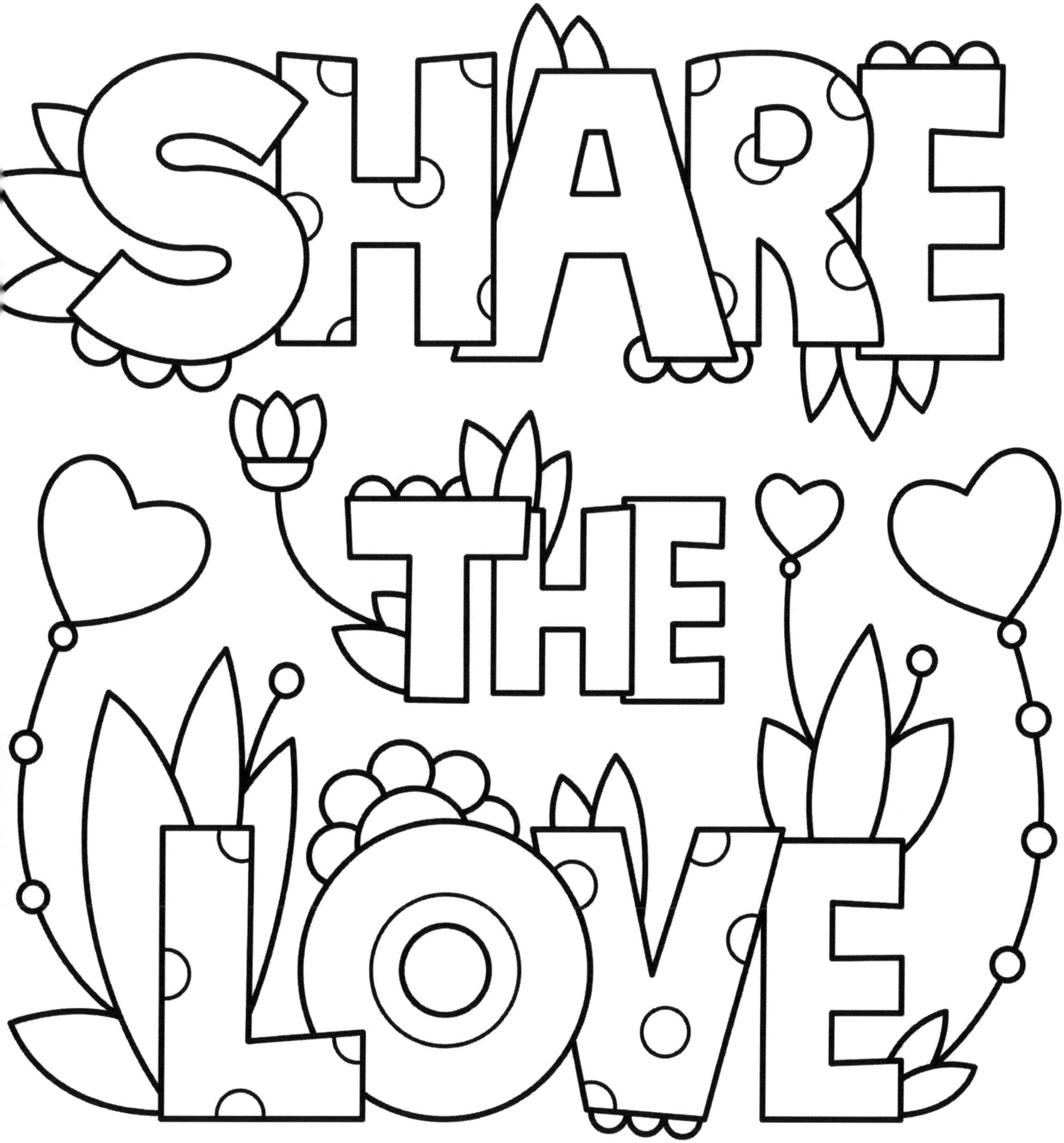
SHARE
THE
LOVE

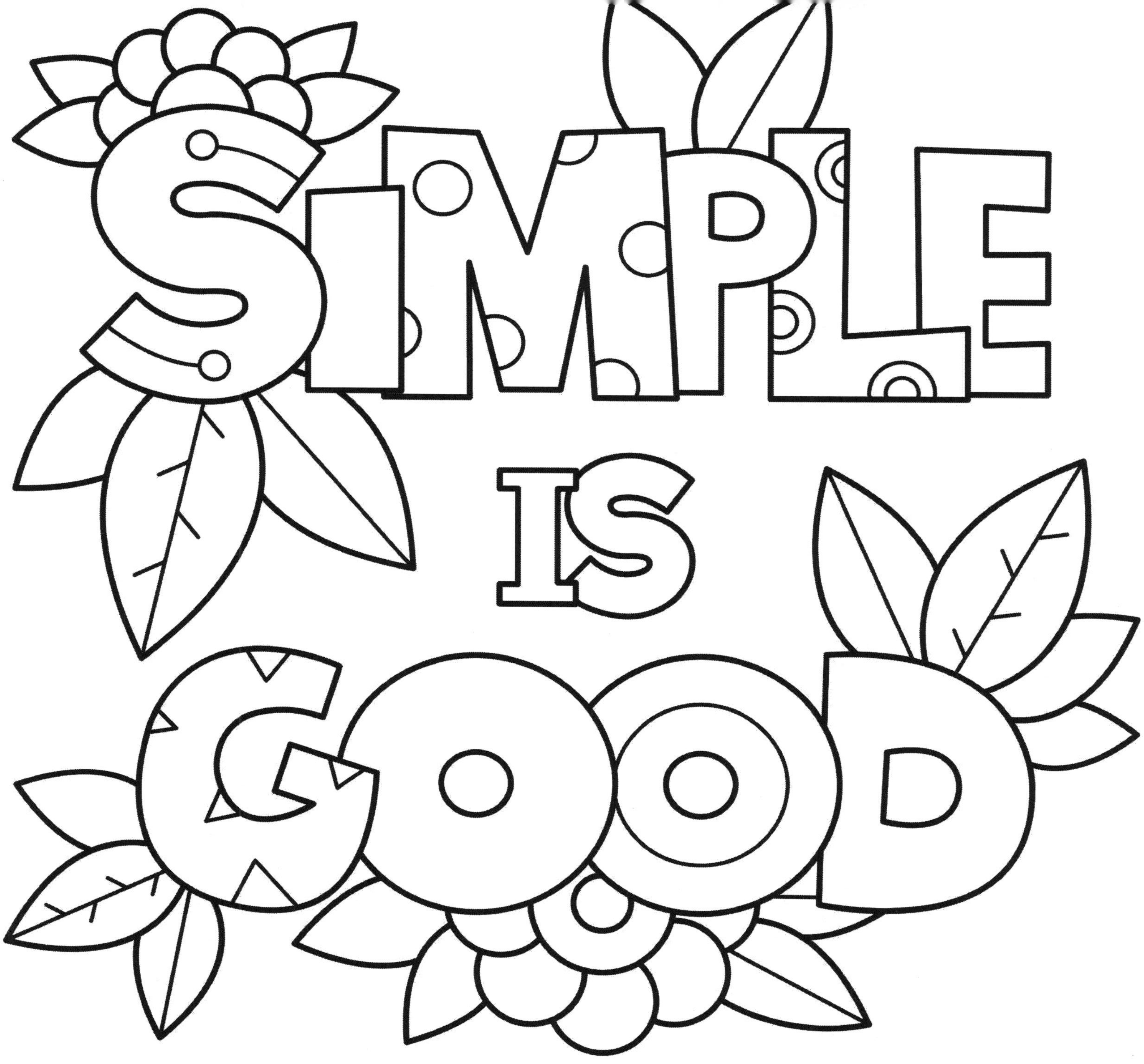
SIMPLE
IS
GOOD

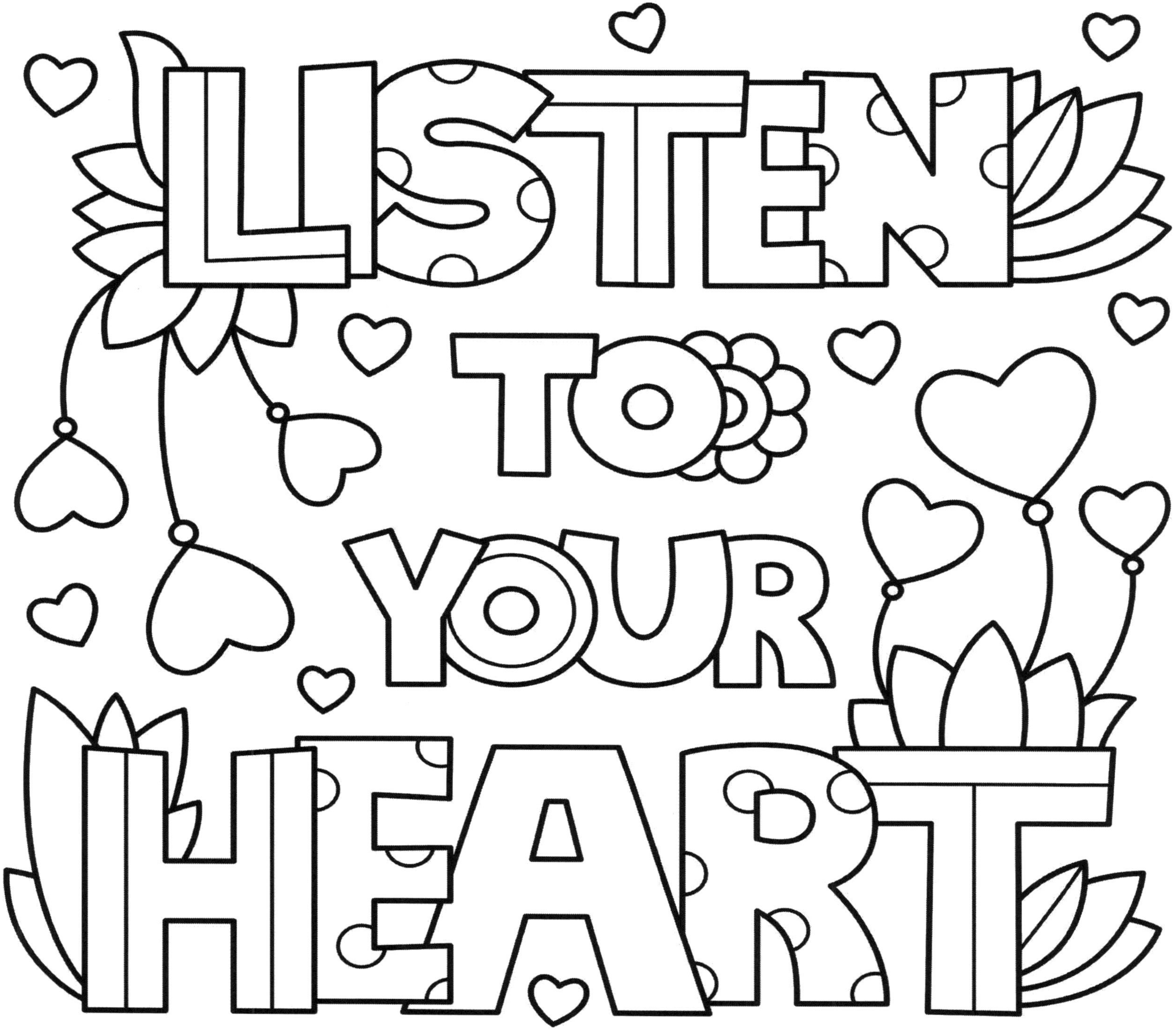
LISTEN TO YOUR HEART

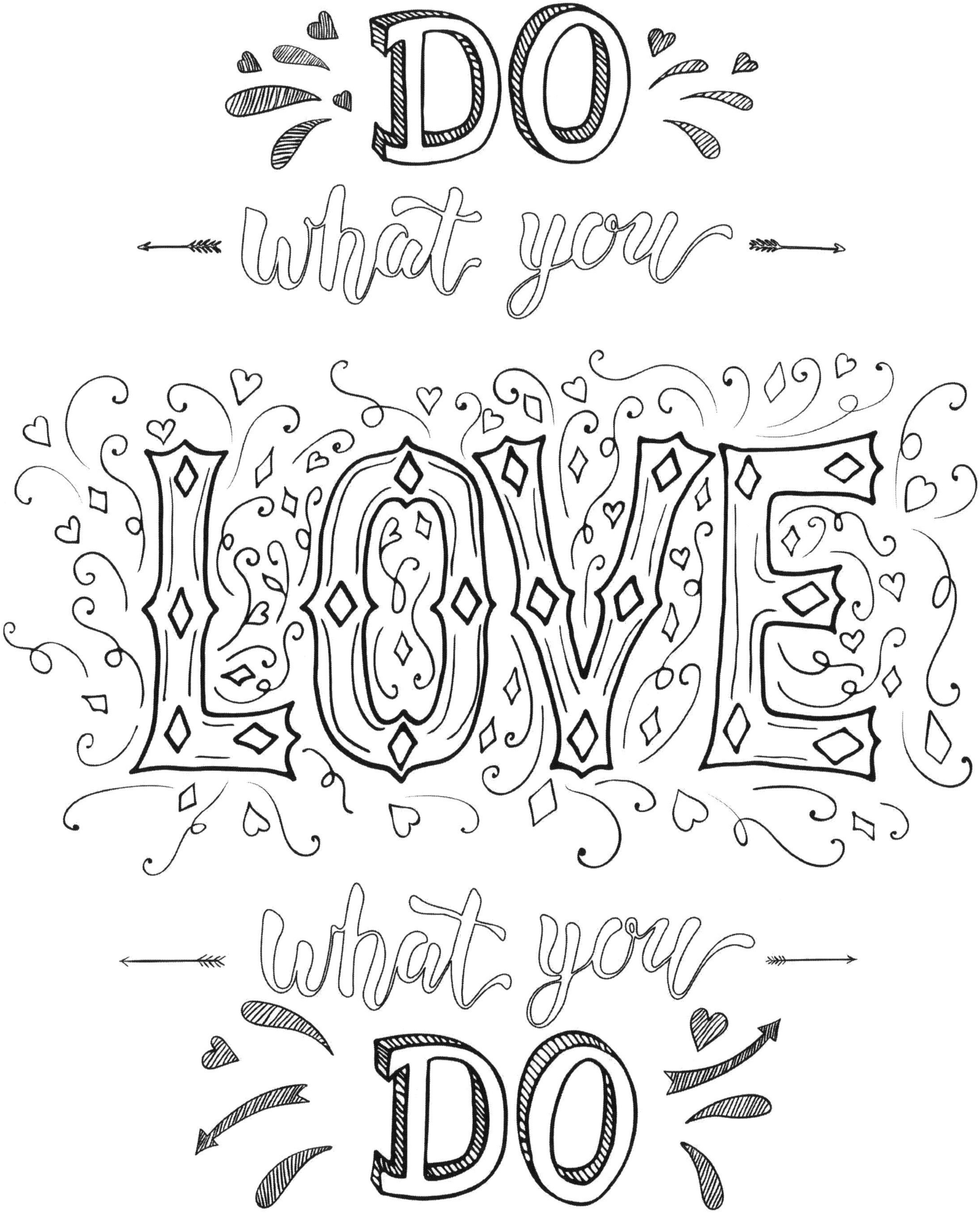
DO
what you
LOVE
what you
DO

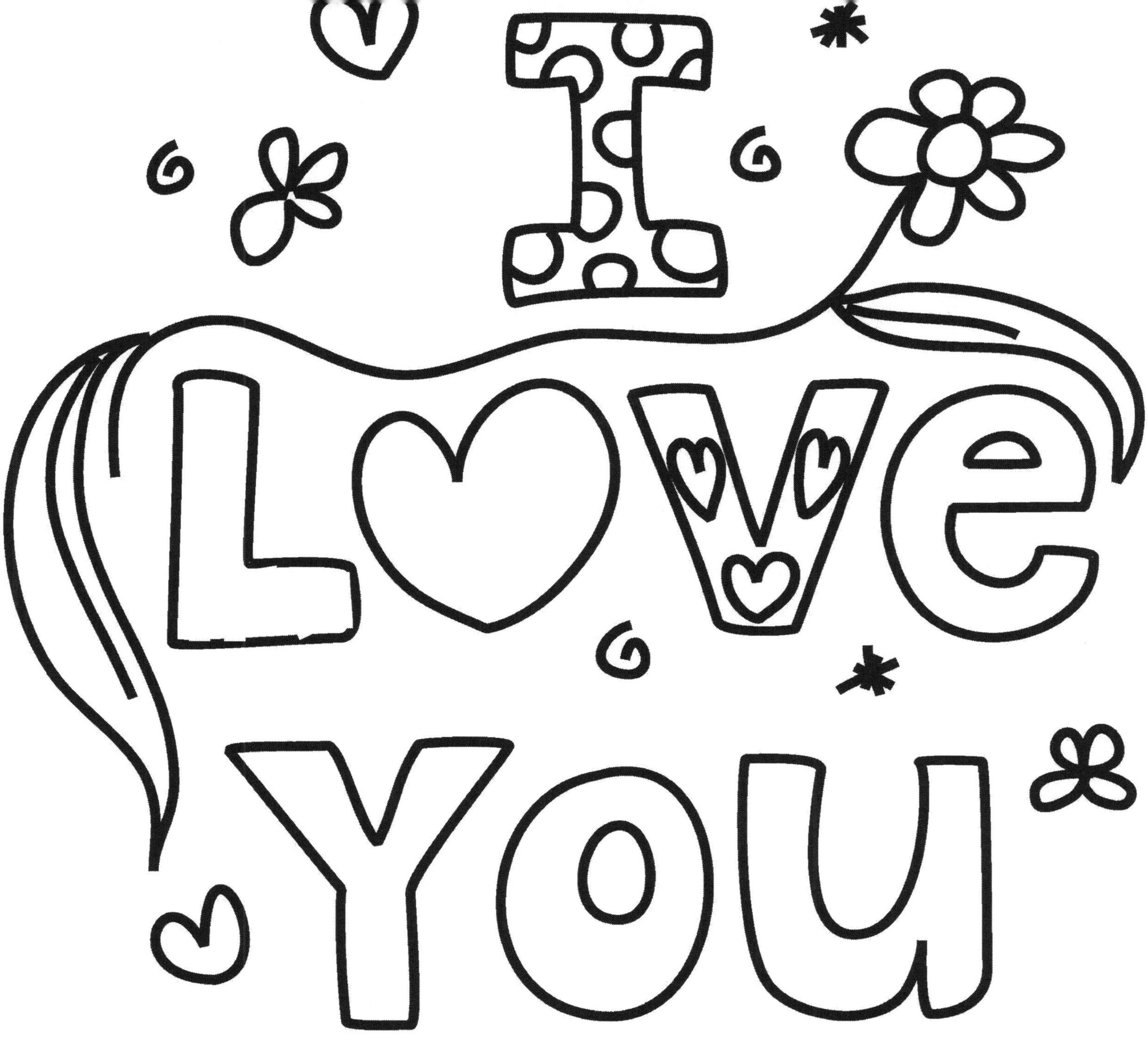
I Love You

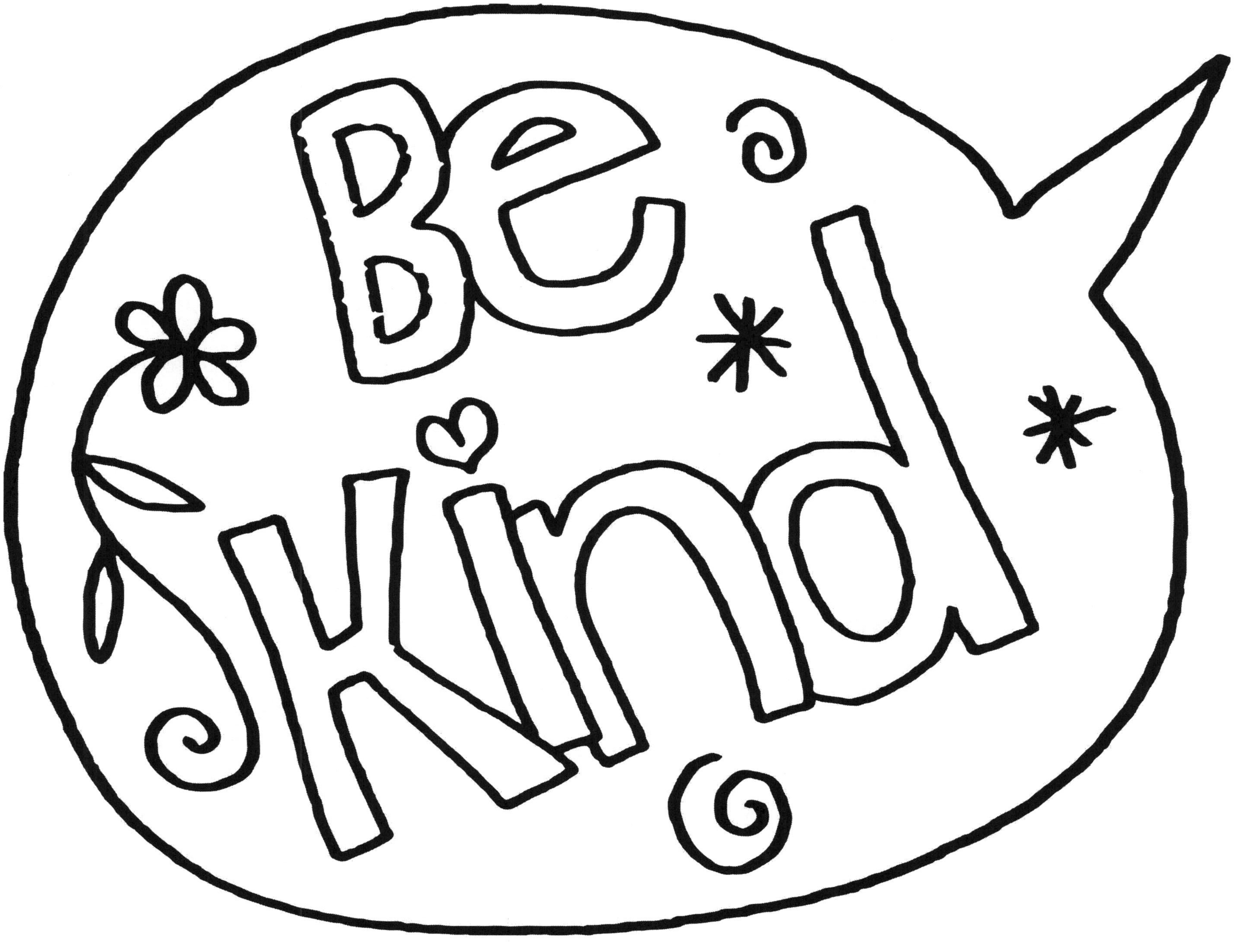
Be Kind

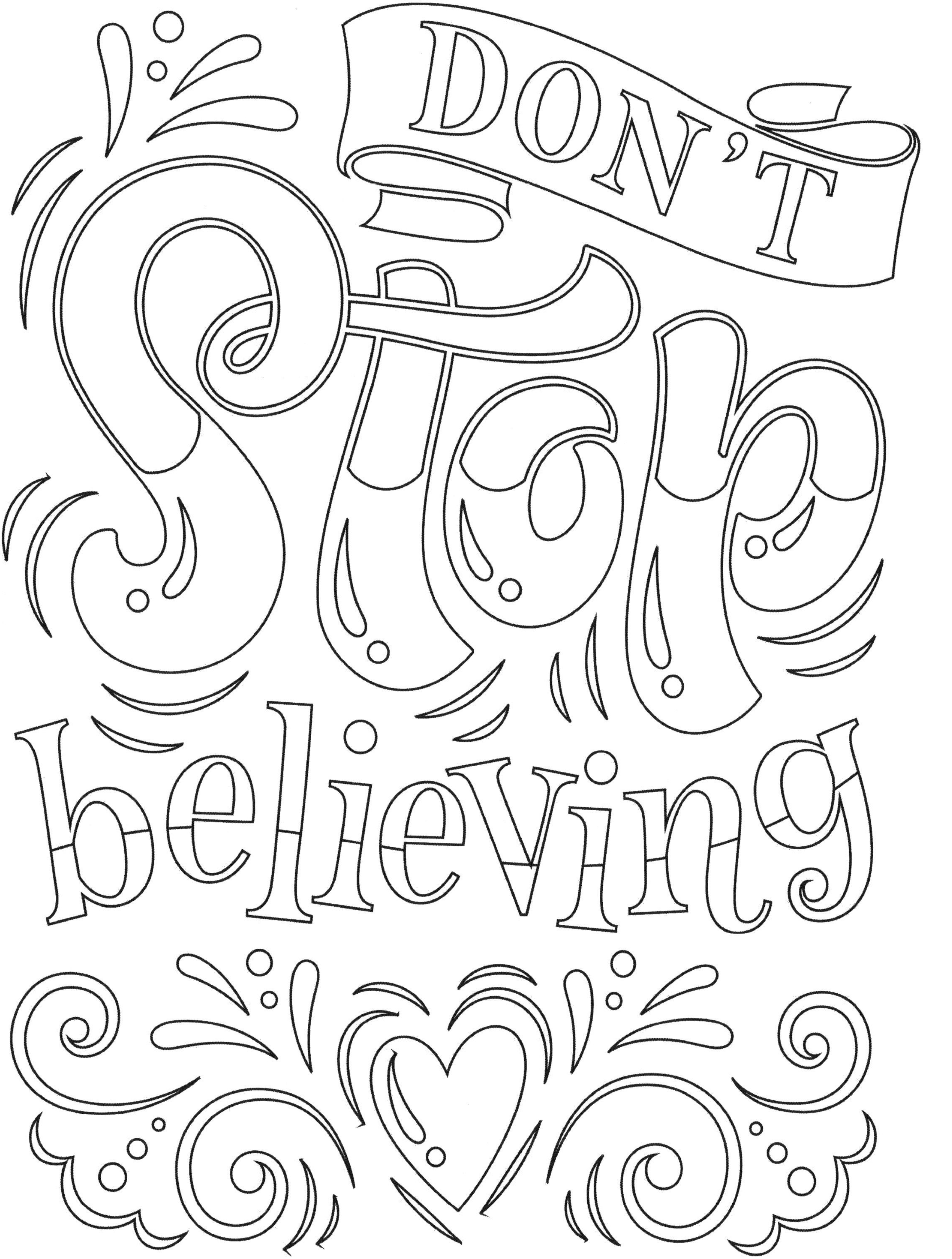
DON'T
Stop
believing

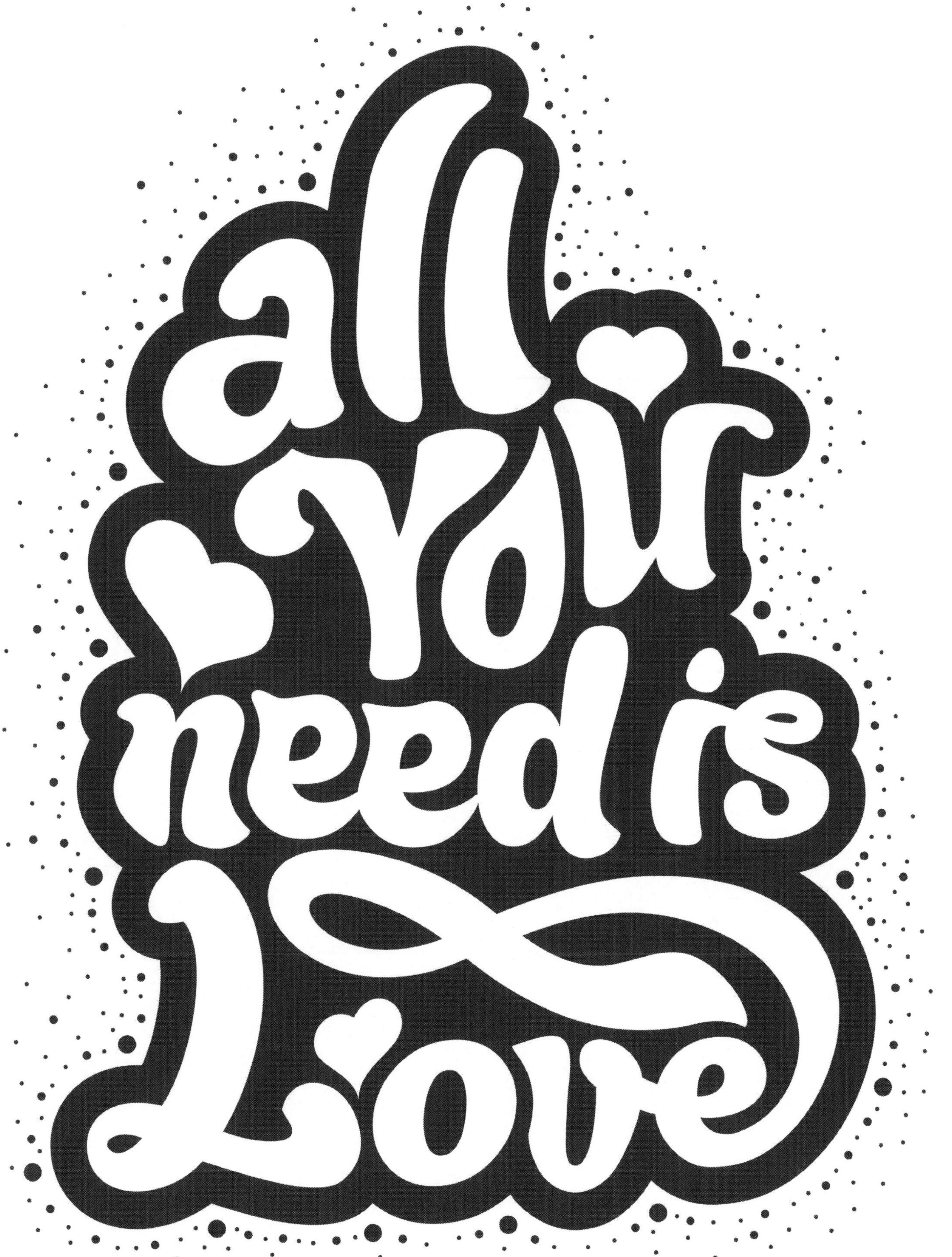
all you need is Love

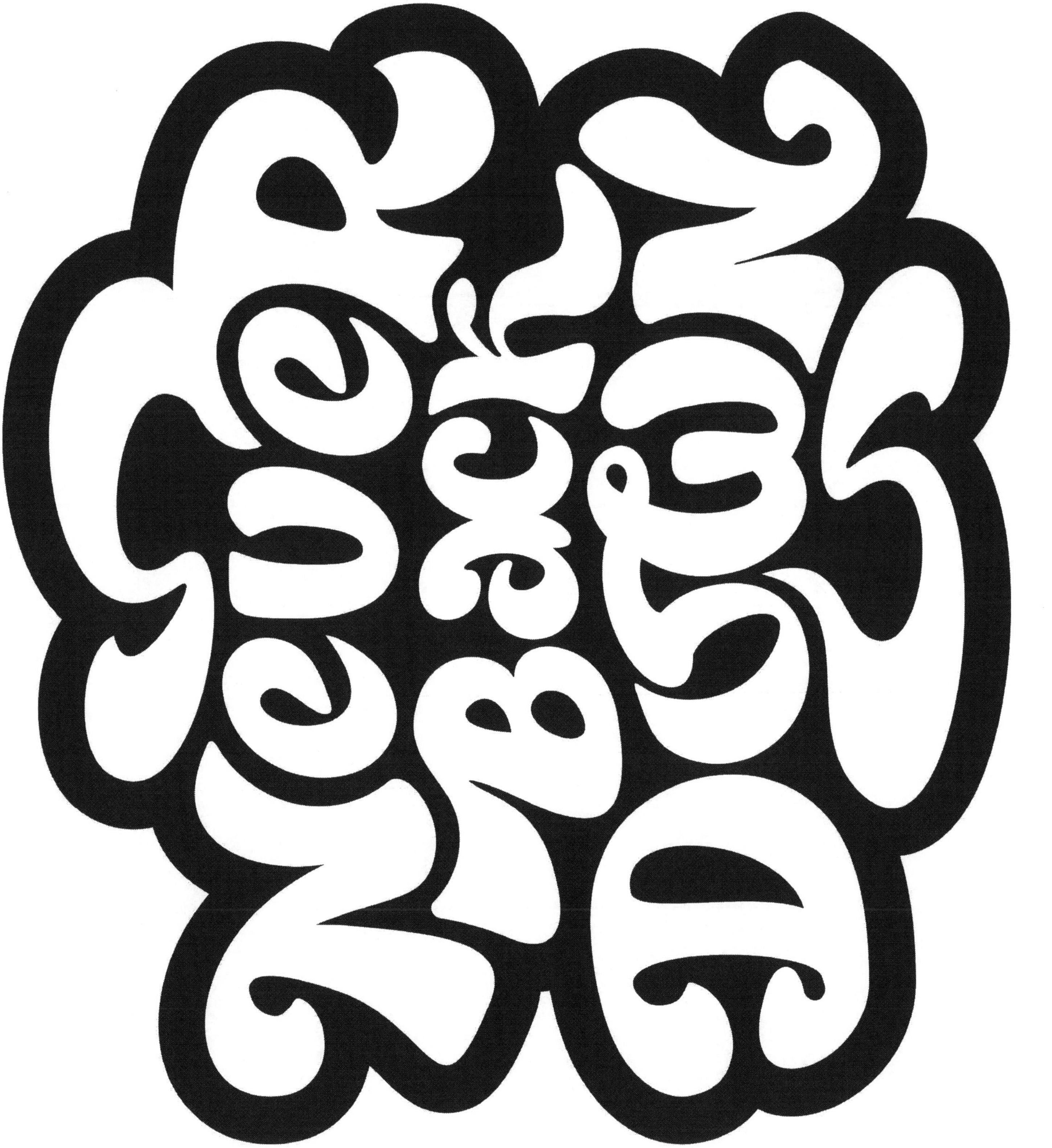

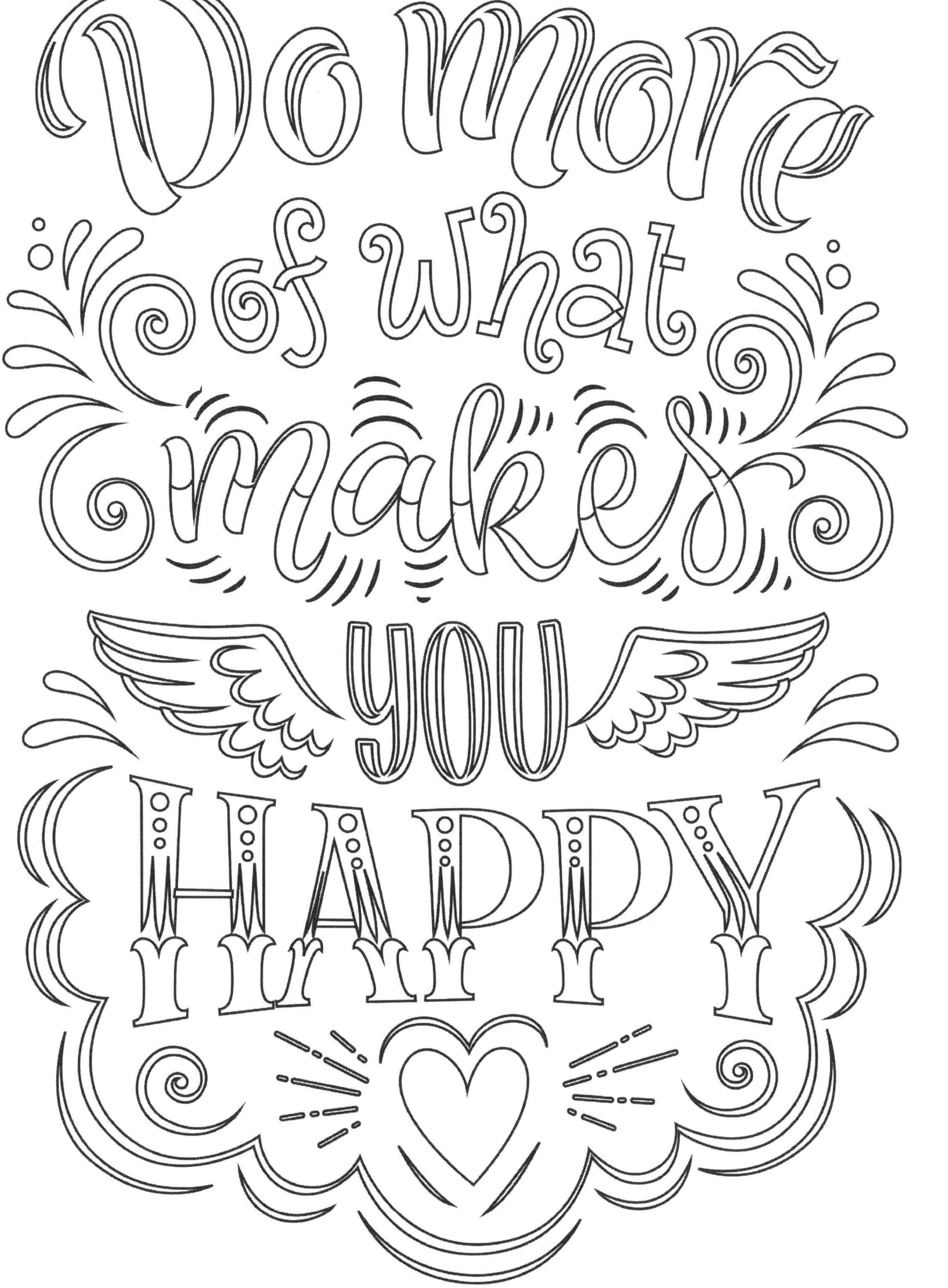
Do more
of what
makes
you
HAPPY

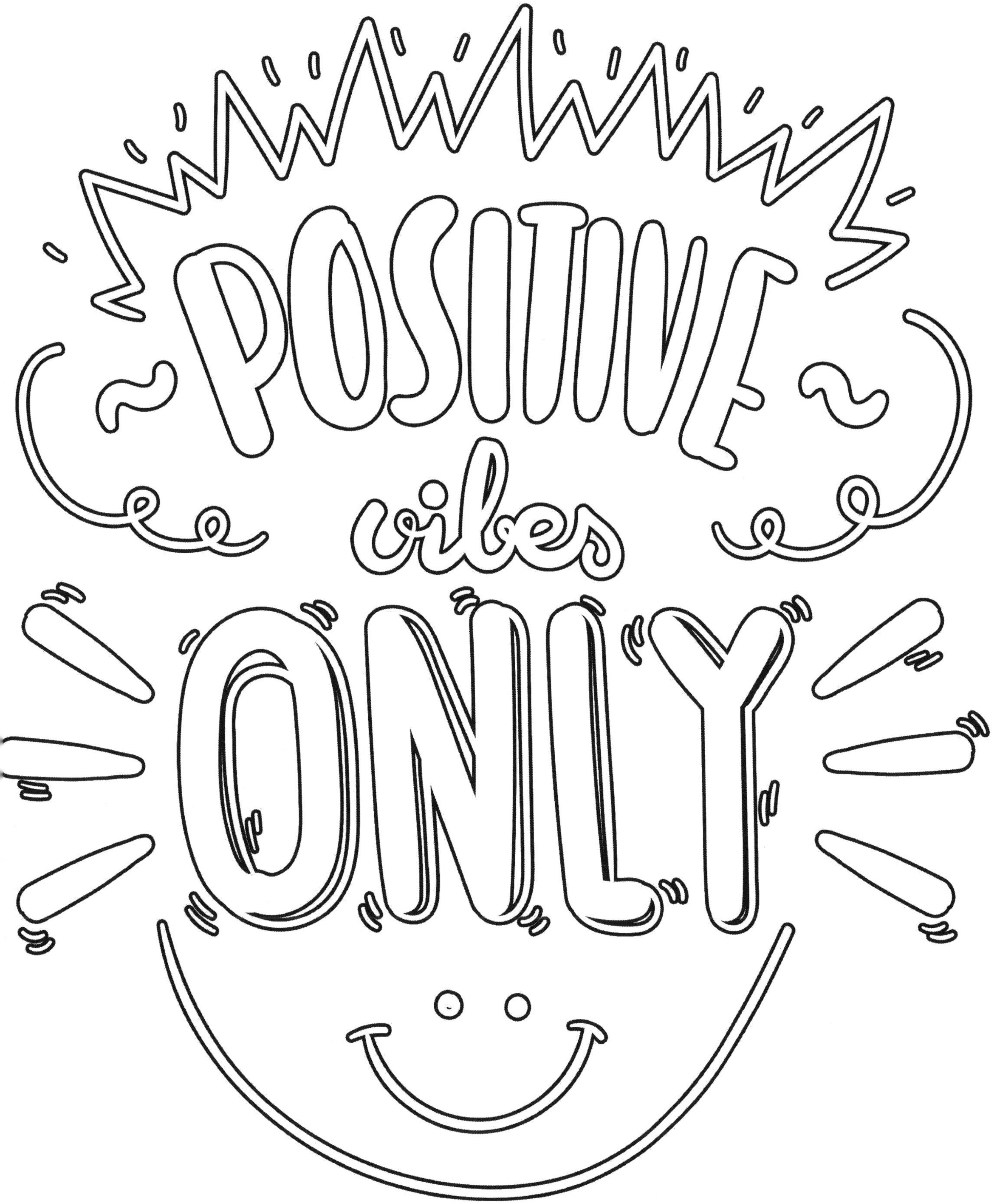
POSITIVE
vibes
ONLY

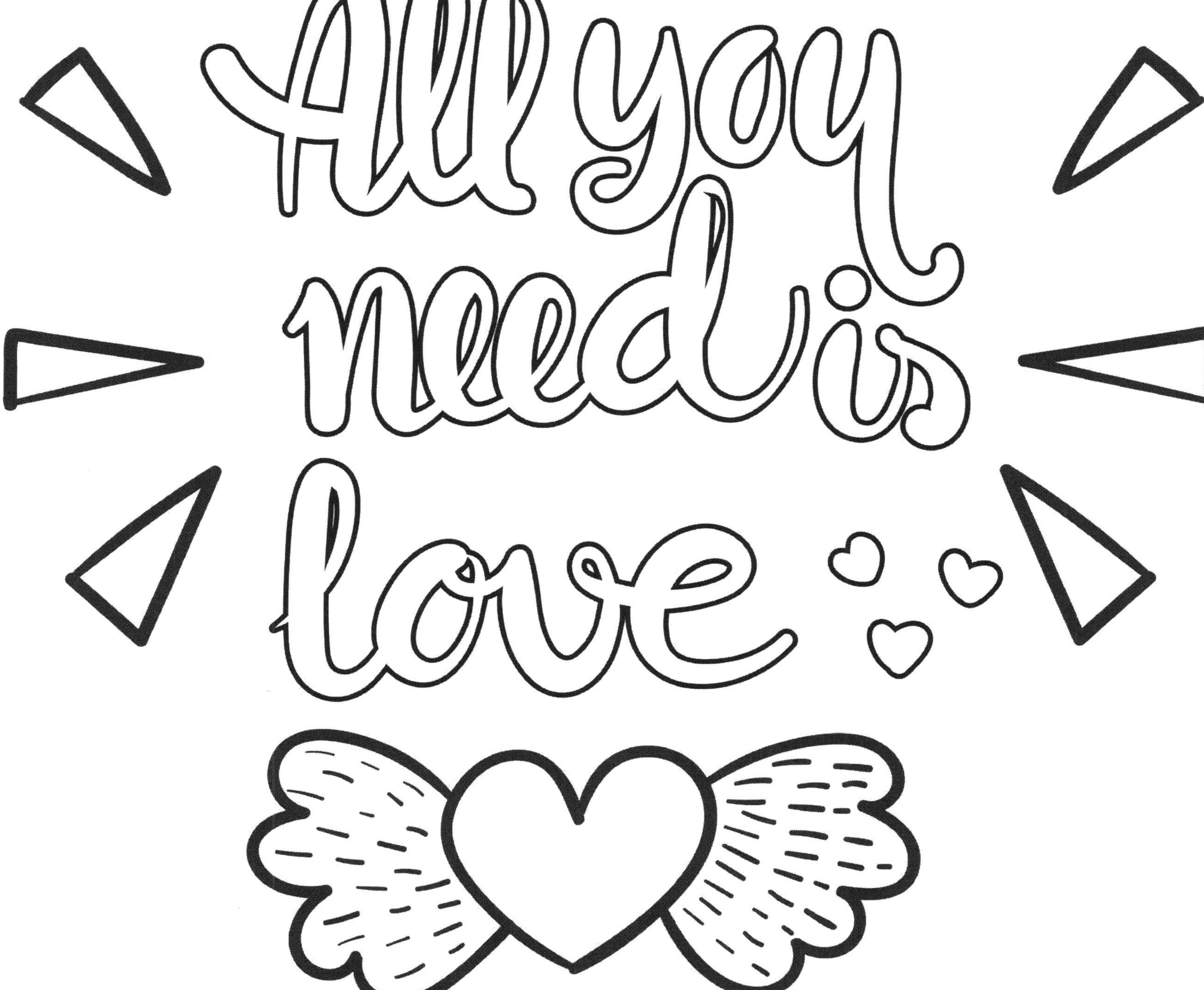
All you
need is
love

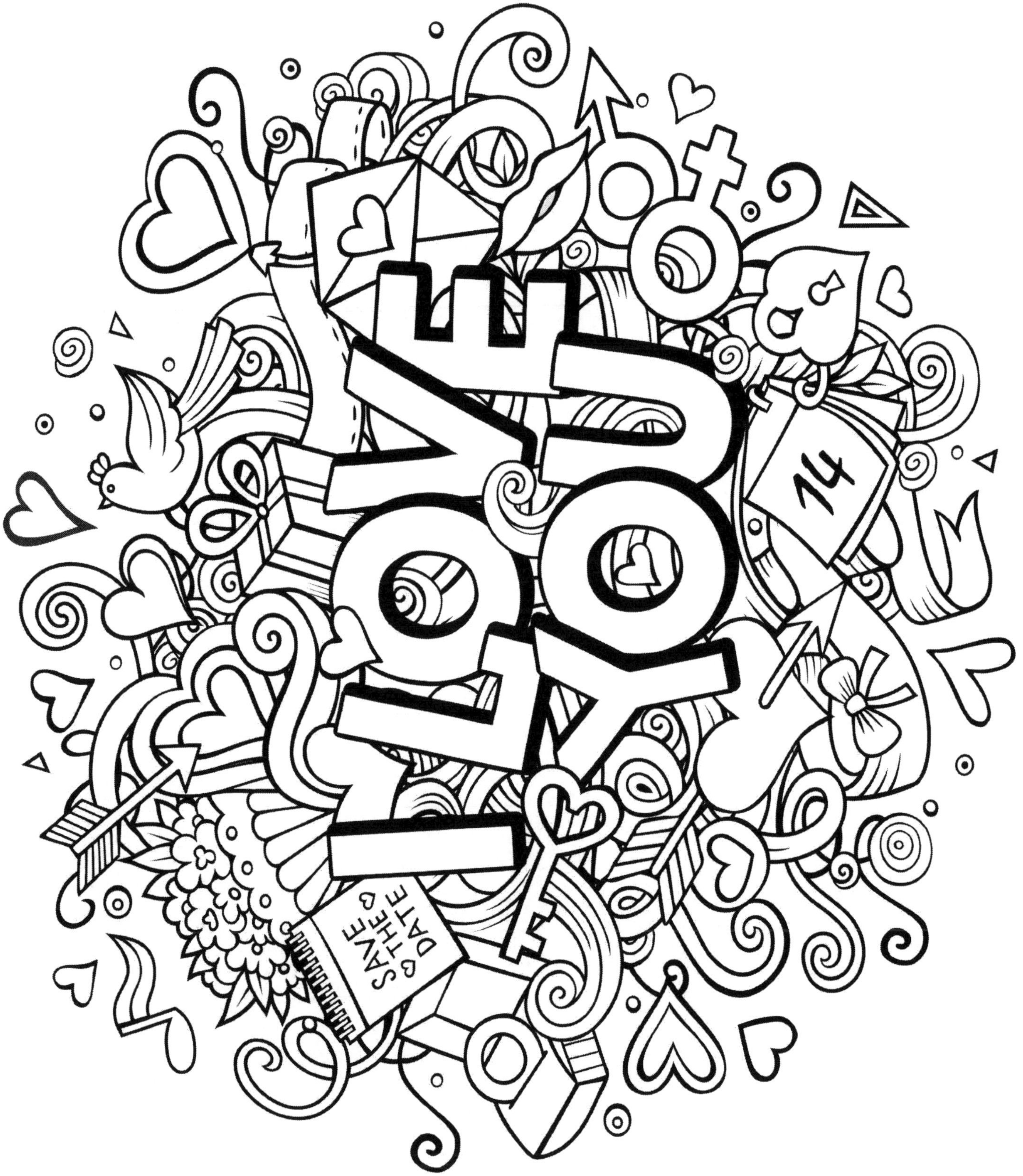
I LOVE YOU
14
SAVE THE DATE

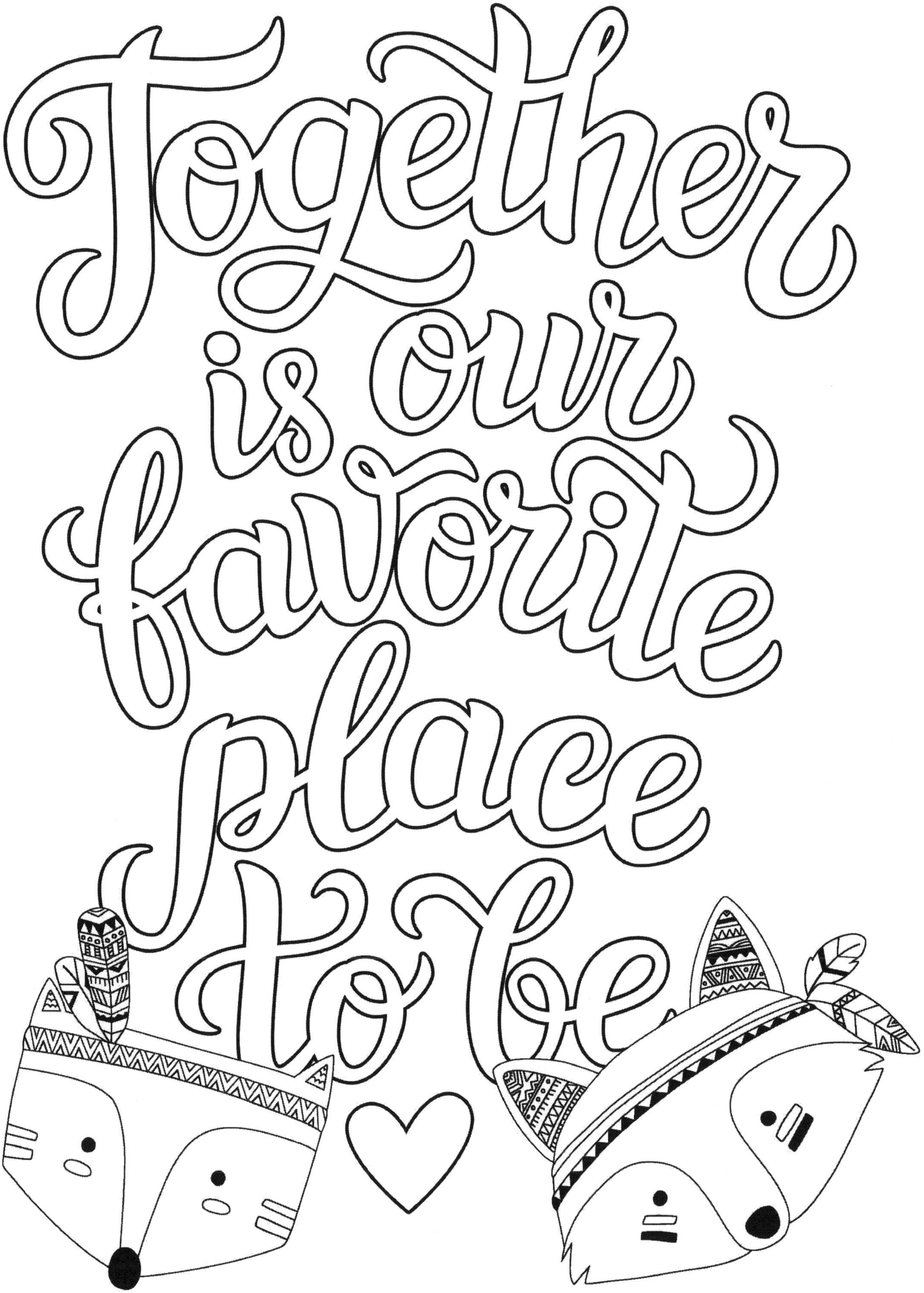
Together
is our
favorite
place
to be

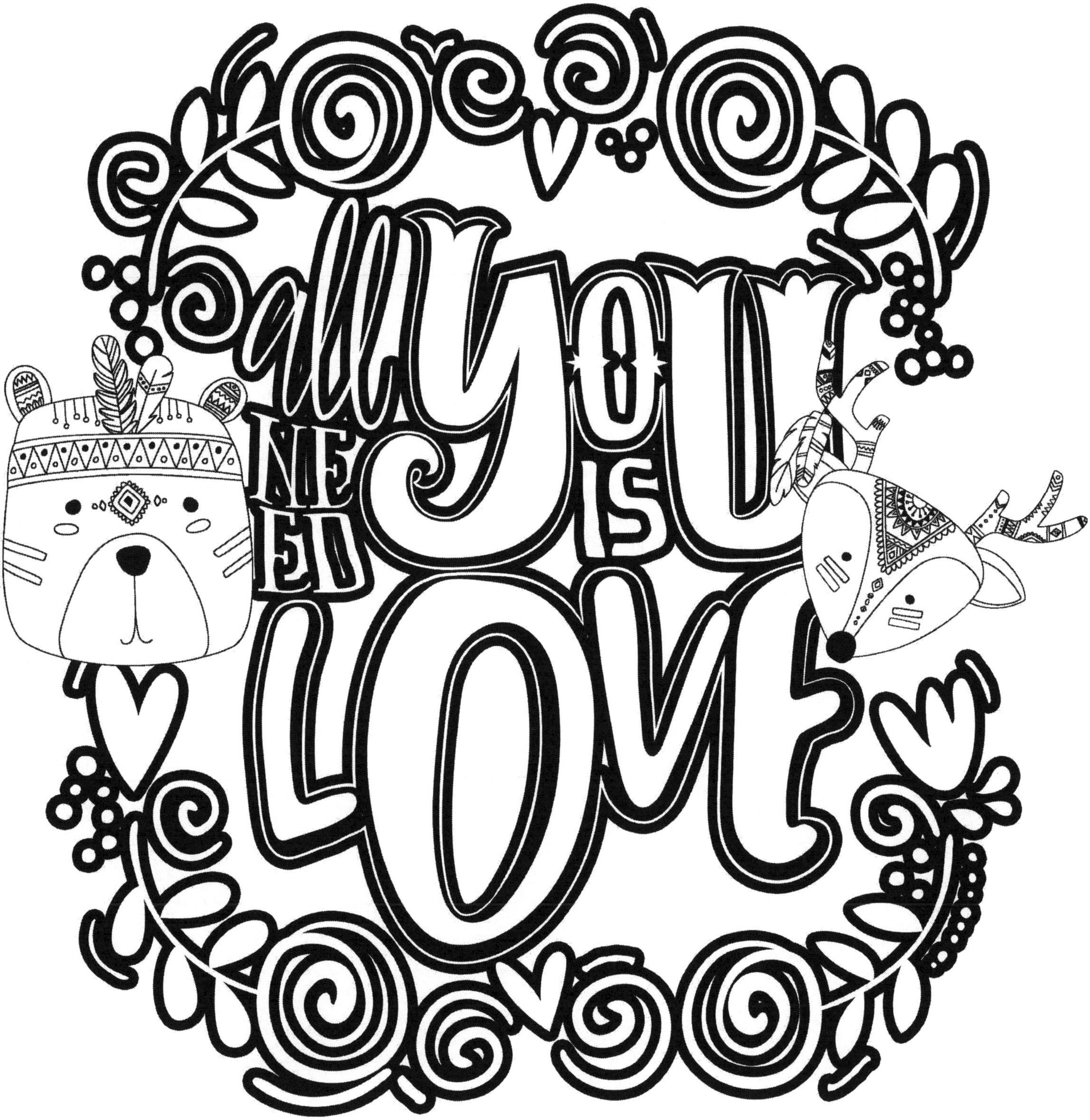
all you need is love

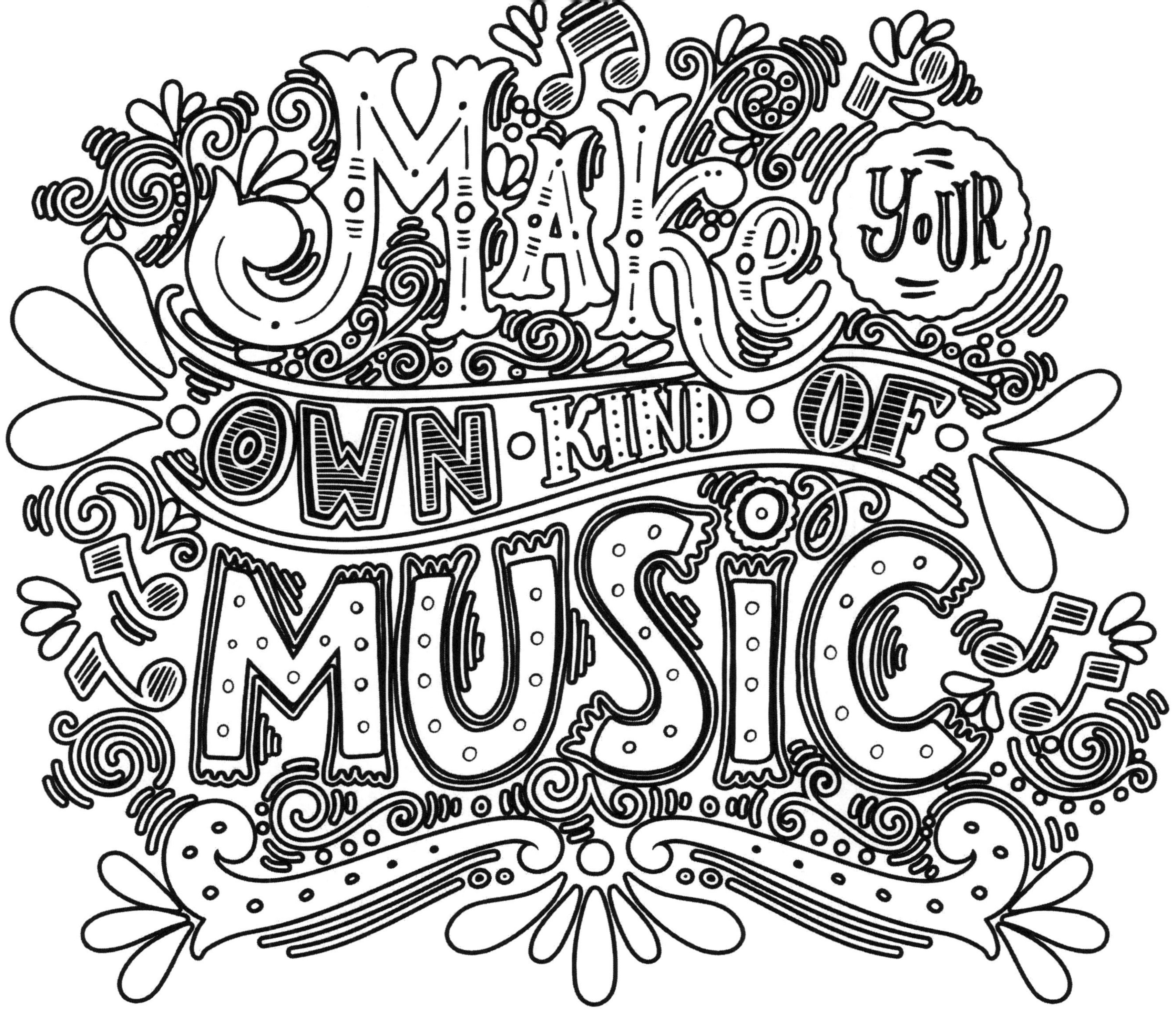
MAKE YOUR
OWN KIND OF
MUSIC

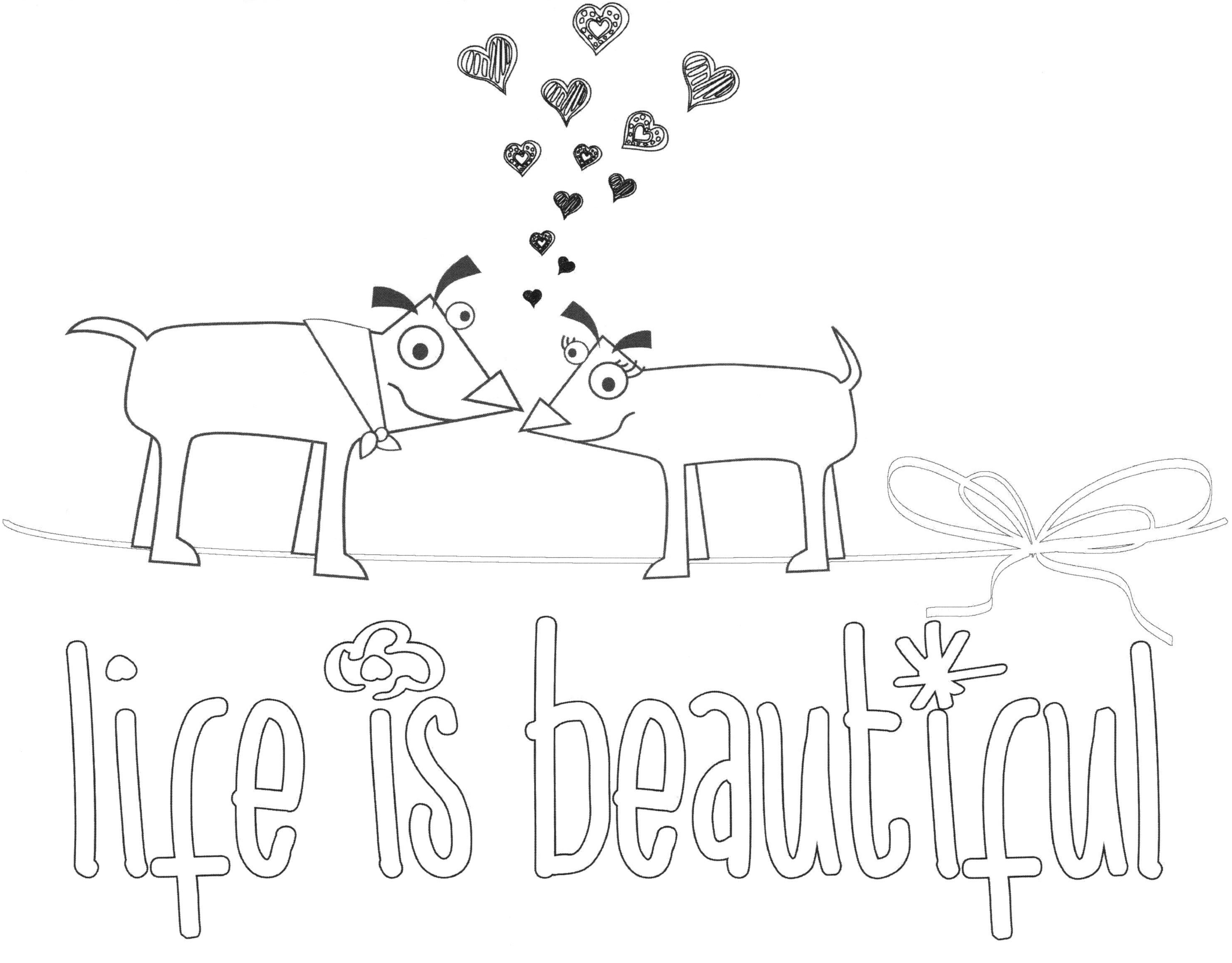
life is beautiful

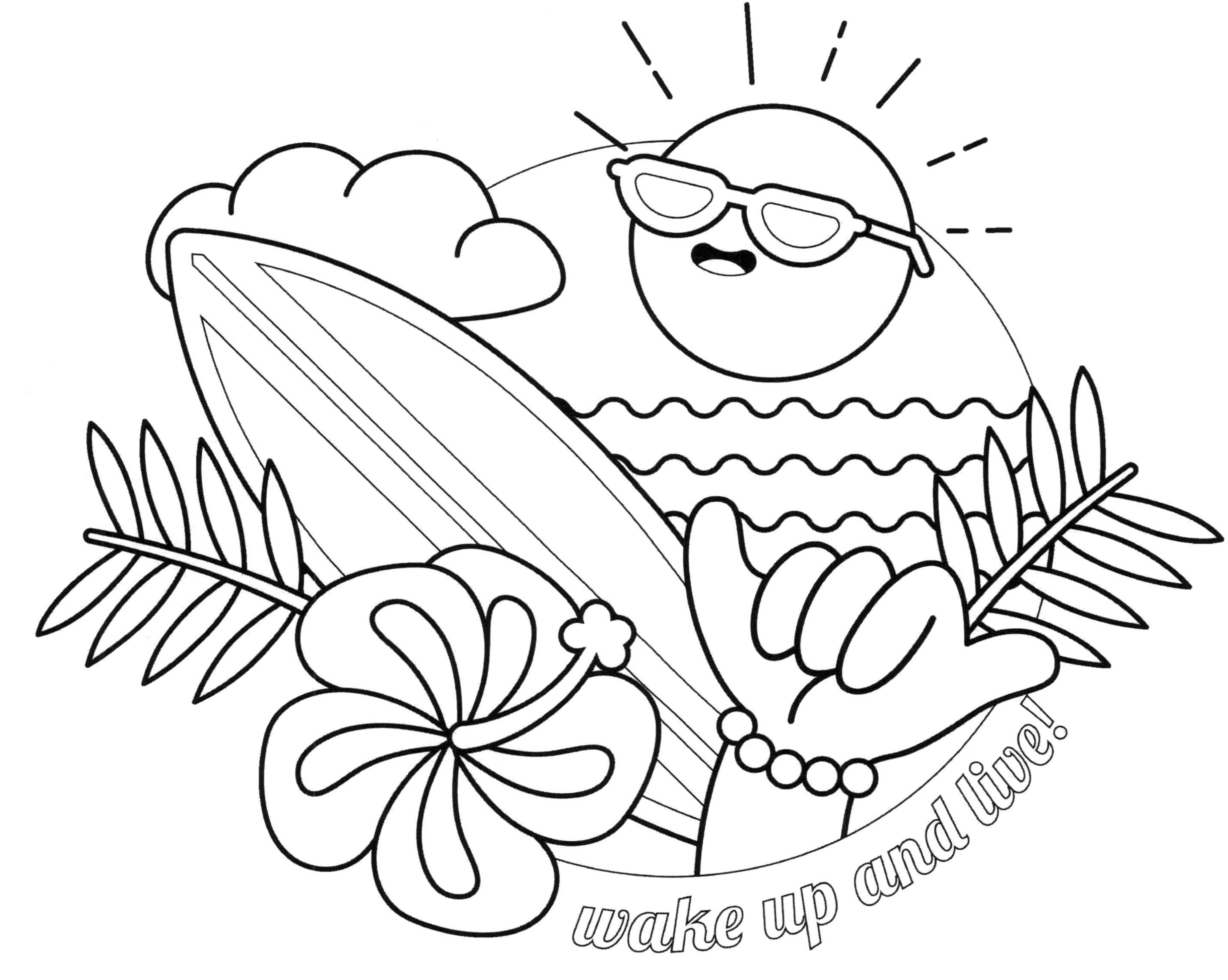
wake up and live!

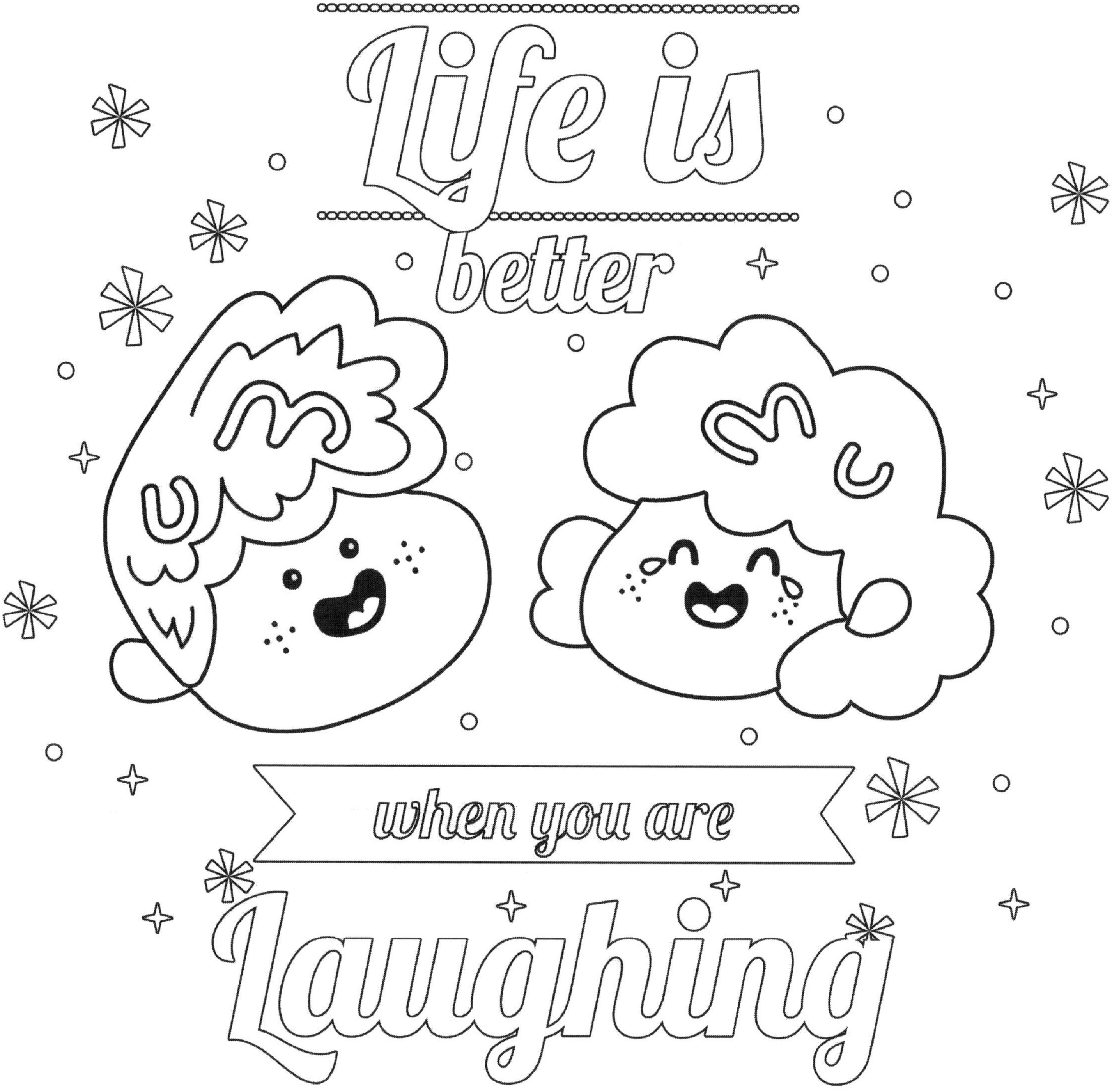
Life is
better
when you are
Laughing

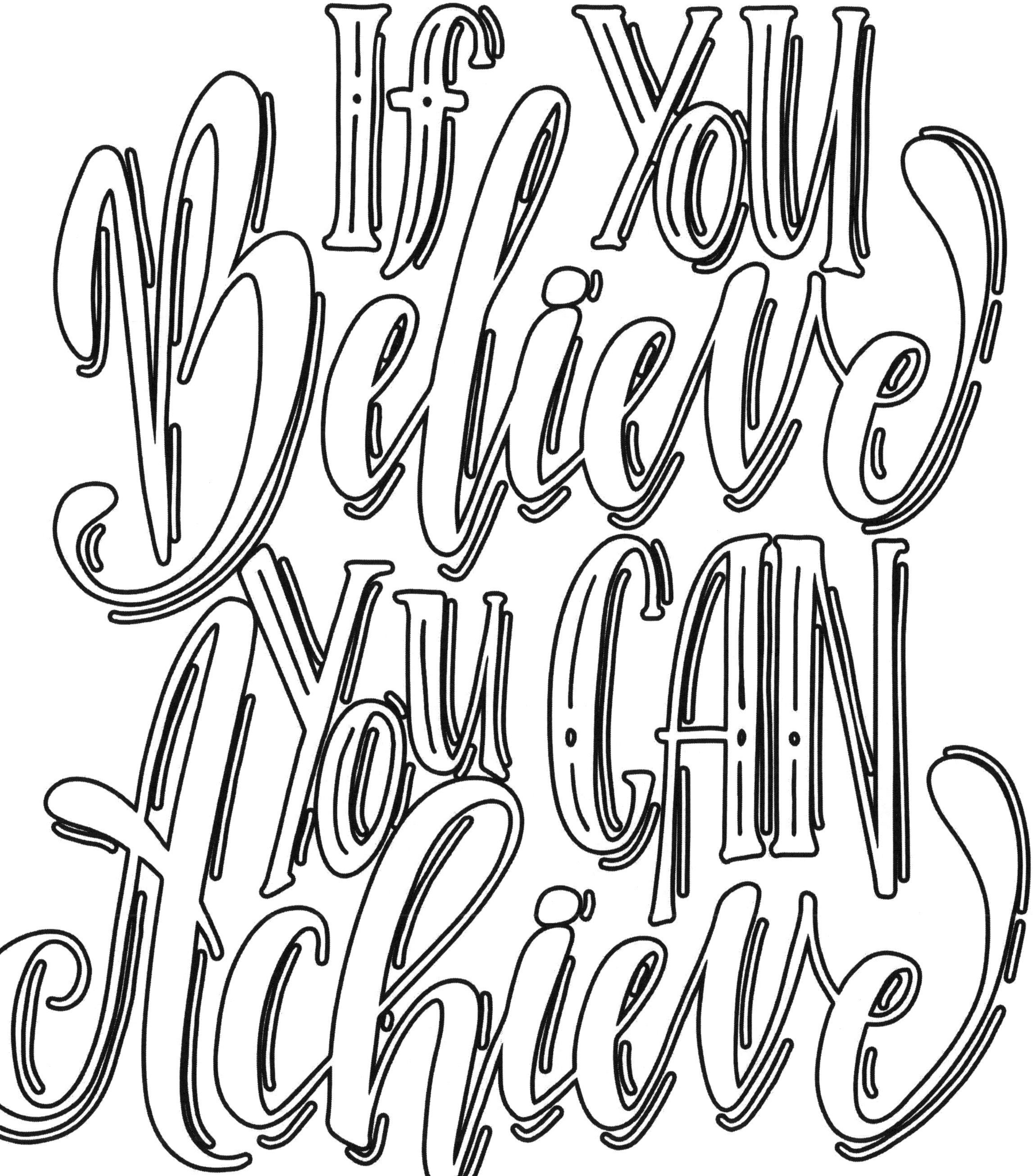
If You
Believe
You CAN
Achieve

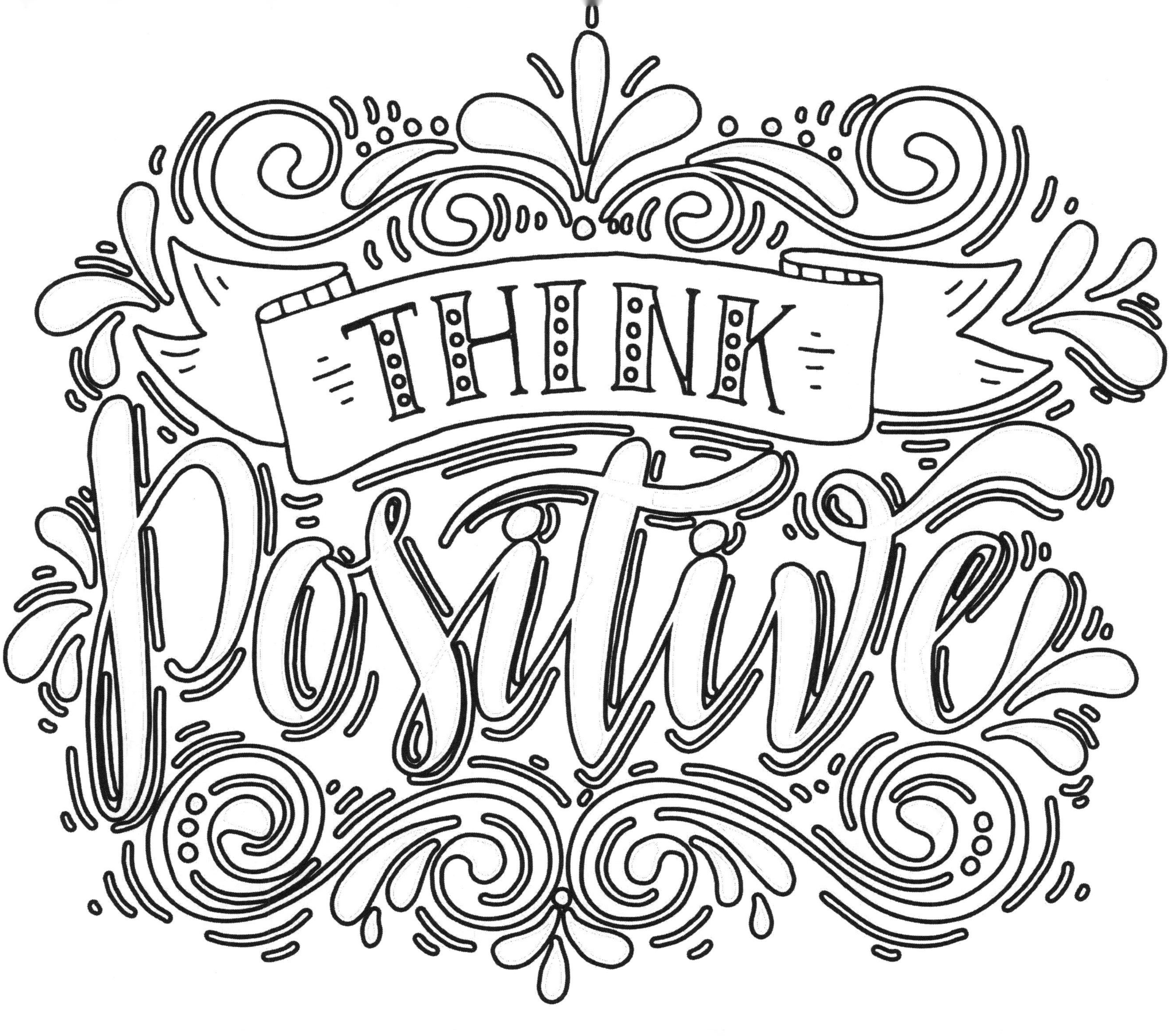
THINK
Positive

14597475R00037

Made in the USA
Lexington, KY
09 November 2018